AF480037

ABC's Just For You

A Journey Through The Alphabet

Paul
Kavanagh

Dedicated To:

My kids and grandkids, Your kids and grandkids, and Everyone else's kids, too.

ABCDEFGHIJKLM

WORDS WITH Aa

Apple

Alphabet

Abra Cadabra

Age: How Old Are You?

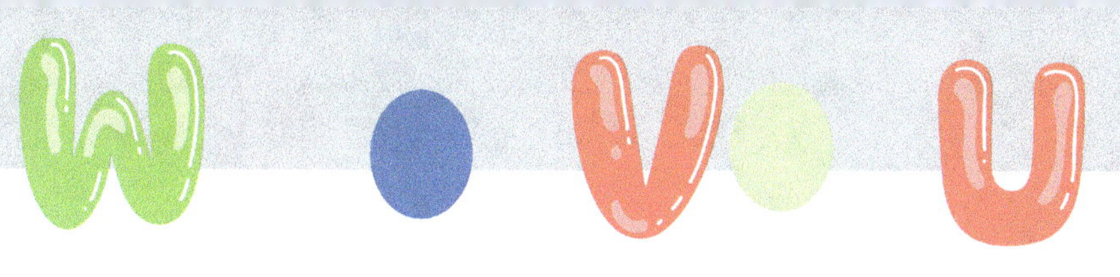

NOPQRSTUVWXYZ

IS FOR

AIRPLANE

WORDS WITH Bb

Bat
Ball
Bike
Banana

NOPQRSTUVWXYZ

IS FOR
BASEBALL

WORDS WITH Cc

Caterpillar
Catastrophe
Candy
Caramel

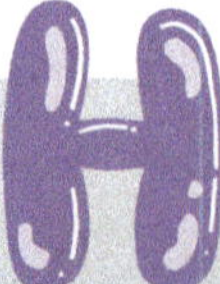

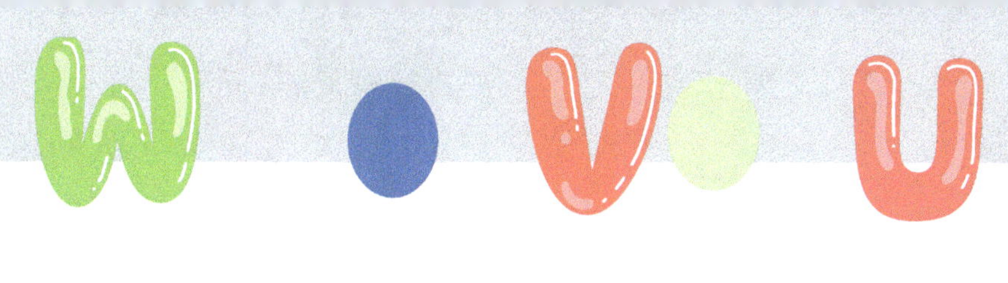

NOPQRSTUVWXYZ

IS FOR

CAR

ABCDEFGHIJKLM

Dd

WORDS WITH Dd

Dog

Dig

Drive

Double

NOPQRSTUVWXYZ

IS FOR

DUMP TRUCK

ABCDEFGHIJKLM

Ee

WORDS WITH Ee

Elephant
Electricity
Ear
End

NOPQRSTUVWXYZ
IS FOR
EASTEREGG

ABCDE**F**GHIJKLM

WORDS WITH Ff

Father
Foot
Far
Funny

NOPQRSTUVWXYZ

IS FOR
FOOTBALL

ABCDEF**G**HIJKLM

WORDS WITH Gg

Green

Golf

Garage

Girl

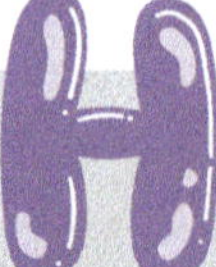

NOPQRSTUVWXYZ

IS FOR

GO-KART

ABCDEFGHIJKLM

Hh

WORDS WITH Hh

Hand

Help

Happy

Hat

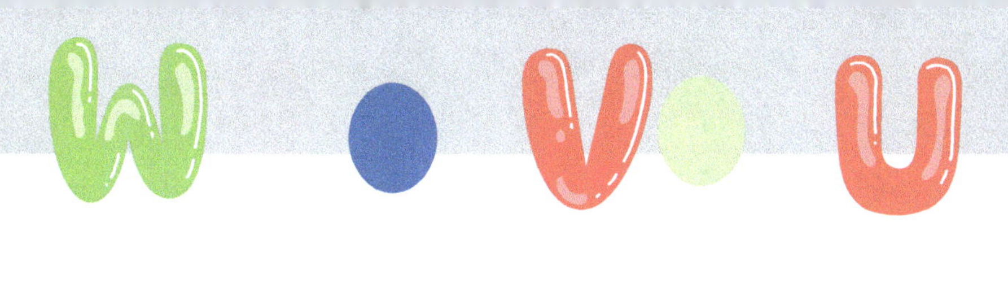

NOPQRSTUVWXYZ

IS FOR

HELICOPTER

WORDS WITH Ii

Ice

Indian

Inside

Invalid

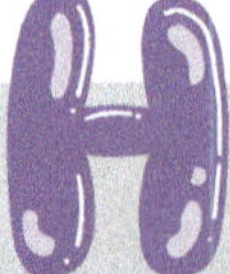

NOPQRSTUVWXYZ

IS FOR
ICE CREAM
CONE

ABCDEFGHIJKLM

Jj

WORDS WITH Jj

Jump

Jacks

Jewel

Jam

NOPQRSTUVWXYZ

IS FOR
JET

WORDS WITH Kk

Karate
Kangaroo
Kayak
Knife

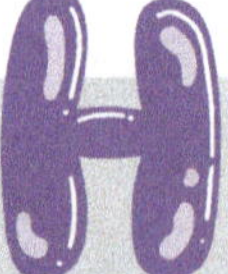

NOPQRSTUVWXYZ
IS FOR
KETCH-UP

ABCDEFGHIJKLM

Ll

WORDS WITH Ll

Leg
Laser
Left
Lose

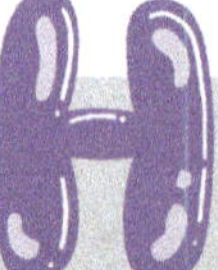

NOPQRSTUVWXYZ

IS FOR

LOCK

ABCDEFGHIJKLM

Mm

WORDS WITH Mm

Mother

Miracle

Mirage

Move

NOPQRSTUVWXYZ

IS FOR

MOTOR

CYCLE

ABCDEFGHIJKLM

Nn

WORDS WITH Nn

Noodle

No

Never

Nap

NOPQRSTUVWXYZ

IS FOR

NOSE

WORDS WITH Oo

Orange

Orangatang

Over

Out

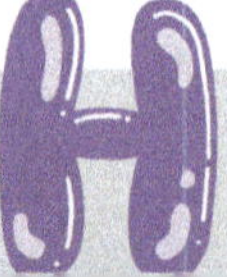

NOPQRSTUVWXYZ

IS FOR
OLD GLORY

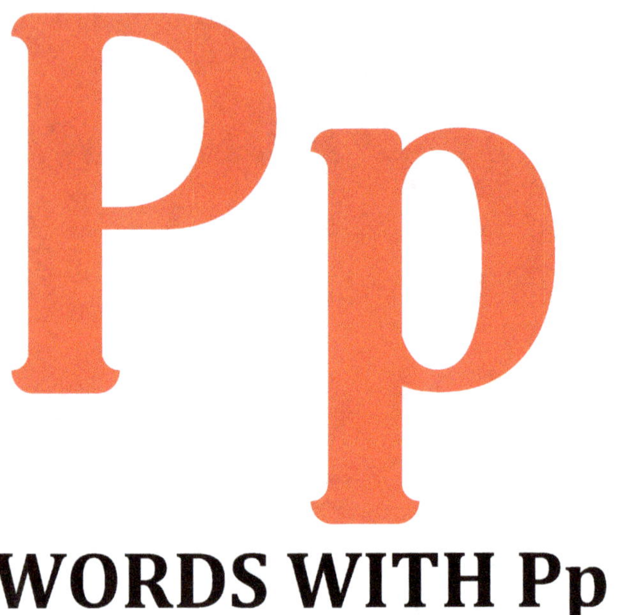

WORDS WITH Pp

People

Pop

Plumb

Place

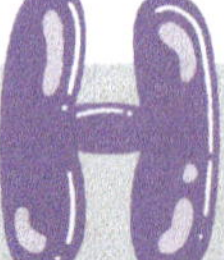

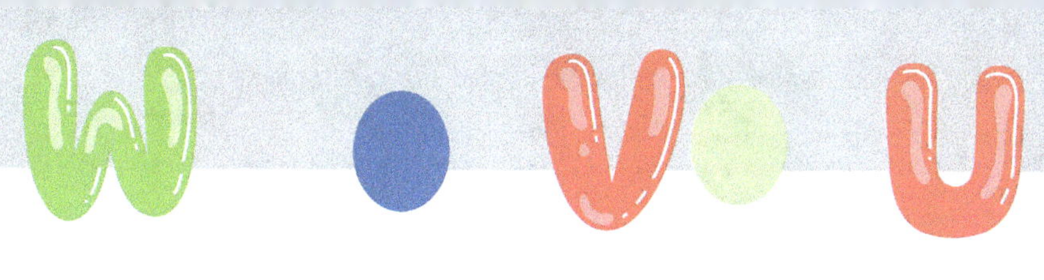

IS FOR

PEPPERONI

PIZZA

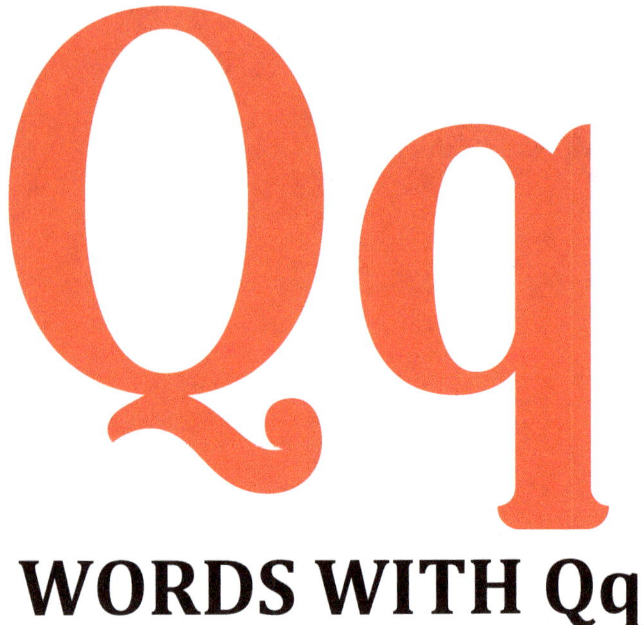

WORDS WITH Qq

Quiet

Queen

Quick

Queue

NOPQRSTUVWXYZ

IS FOR

QUICK-SAND

ABCDEFGHIJKLM

WORDS WITH Rr

Real

Raft

Right

Red

NOPQRSTUVWXYZ

IS FOR

ROBOT

WORDS WITH Ss

Seven

Strike

Stick

Sell

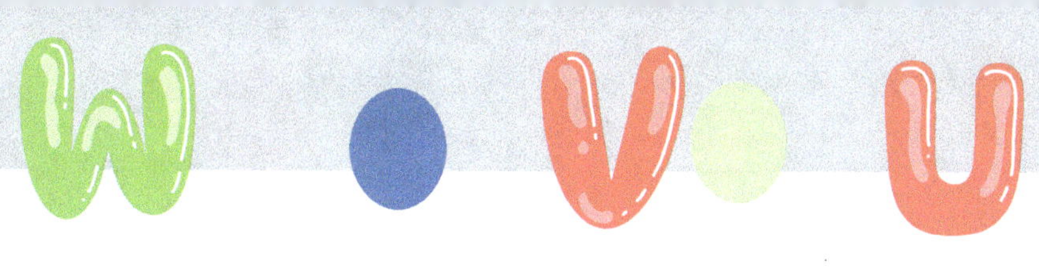

IS FOR STEAM-ROLLER

ABCDEFGHIJKLM

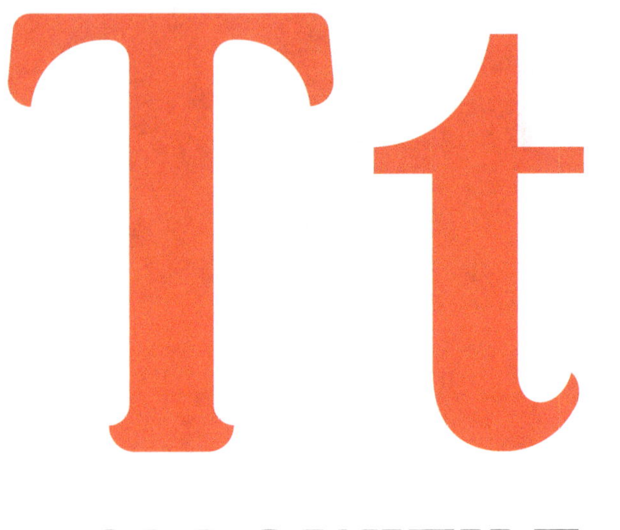

Tt

WORDS WITH Tt

Two
Three
Ten
Tree

NOPQRSTUVWXYZ

IS FOR

TRICYCLE

WORDS WITH Uu

Under

Umpire

Union

Ugly

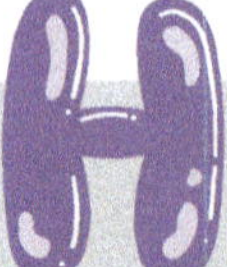

NOPQRSTUVWXYZ
IS FOR
UNITED
STATES

ABCDEFGHIJKLM

WORDS WITH Vv

Vampire

Very

Veal

Victory

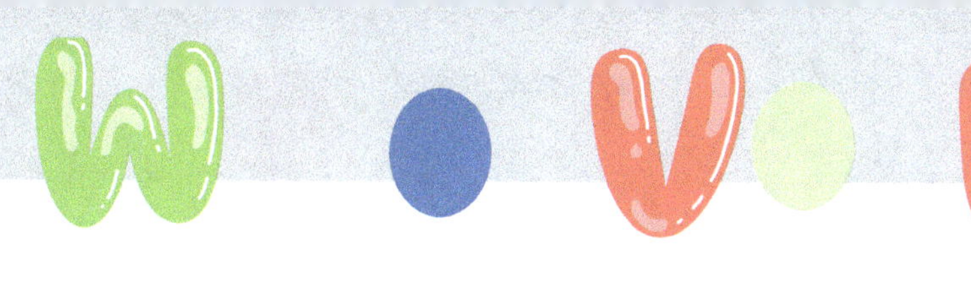

NOPQRSTU**V**WXYZ

IS FOR
VAGABOND

ABCDEFGHIJKLM

WORDS WITH Ww

Will

Way

Wrong

Wind

NOPQRSTUV**W**XYZ

IS FOR
WHEELIE

ABCDEFGHIJKLM

WORDS WITH Xx

Xenon

Xylophone

Xerox

Xanthan

NOPQRSTUVW**X**YZ

IS FOR
X-RAY GUN

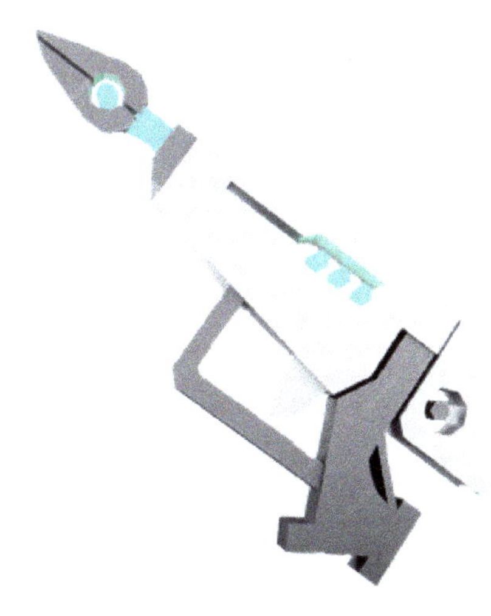

ABCDEFGHIJKLM

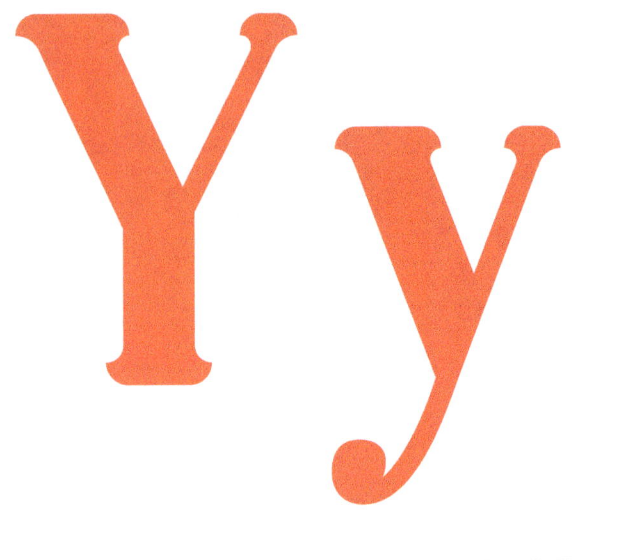

WORDS WITH Yy

Yellow
Yummy
Yuck
Yacht

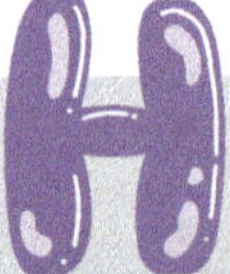

NOPQRSTUVWX**Y**Z

IS FOR

YOU

ABCDEFGHIJKLM

WORDS WITH Zz

Zoo

Zoom

Zig-Zag

zip

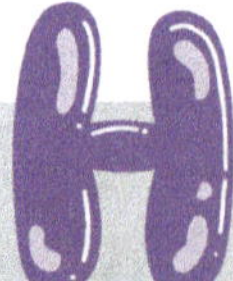

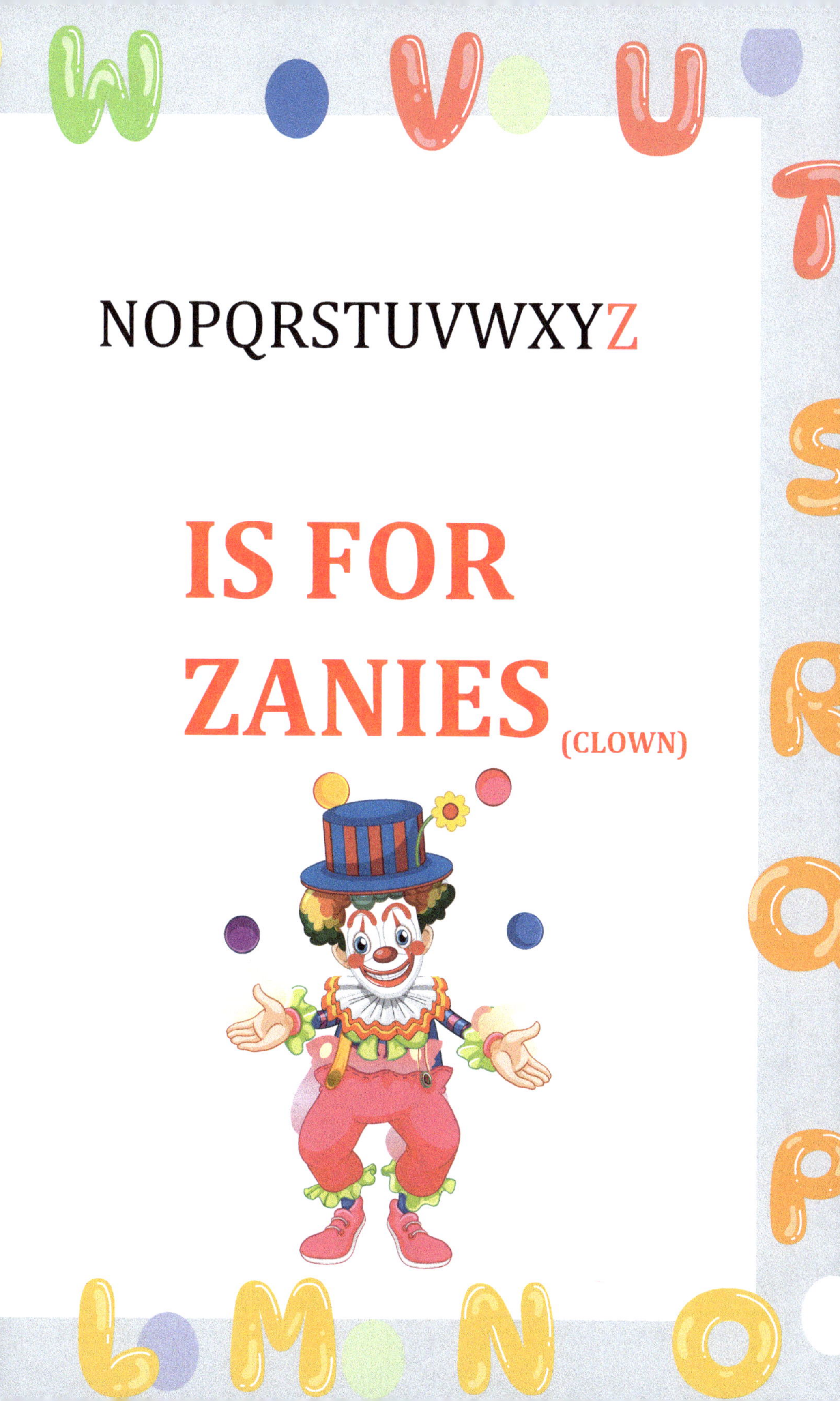

NOPQRSTUVWXYZ
IS FOR
ZANIES
(CLOWN)